FABRIC

FABRIC

PRELUDES TO THE LAST AMERICAN BOOK

RICHARD FROUDE

HORSE LESS PRESS

© 2011 Richard Froude. All rights reserved.

ISBN: 978-0-982989-60-9

Design & typesetting by HR Hegnauer | hrhegnauer.com
Typeset in Cochin.

— — —

Excerpts from this book, often as earlier versions, have first appeared in *The Electronic Drivel Review, Diagram, Parcel, Pop Séance, aPlod, Tarpaulin Sky, Thuggery & Grace, Mirage #4 Periodical, Page Boy, Bombay Gin, Wolf In A Field,* and *Web Conjunctions*. Thanks to the editors of all these publications.

Thank you to all who have supported me through this writing, especially my family; to Bin Ramke and Eleni Sikelianos for their encounters with this text in its formative stages; to Jen Denrow and Jen Tynes for their roles in making this happen; and to Erik Anderson and Selah Saterstrom for their continued belief, advice, and friendship.

For all of these things and more,
this book is for Rohini.

— — —

HORSE LESS PRESS
Denver, Colorado
www.horselesspress.com

Every book is a book of memory. Do we keep the memory of a whole life intact? Of course not. Thus we are the first ones involuntarily to attack duration by fragmenting it, each of its lived moments rising up against the others in the hope of surviving them. Each of those moments is birth and death multiplied, and there is never an established, certified birth or death, but a perpetual displacement of life towards death.

– EDMOND JABÈS

1. TYPE

Memory is a kind / of accomplishment / a sort of renewal

– WILLIAM CARLOS WILLIAMS

— — —

At Bristol Zoo in the mid 1990s I watched an LED display of the world's increasing population. The figure was juxtaposed with the decreasing acreage of rainforest. What I mean is, I am interested in sequence.

I am not certain about the origins of our alphabet. I know that my name begins with the letter R and I was named after nobody in particular. My middle name is my father's name. My father's name is David. St. David is the patron saint of Wales. I don't know what St. David did.

St. George (patron saint of England) killed a dragon. St. George's day is April 23rd, also Shakespeare's birthday and the day on which Shakespeare died. I've often wondered which season I'd prefer to die in. Which day of the week.

— — —

Alfred died in the early hours of New Year's Day, 13 years ago. I was sleeping on the floor of my cousin's room, had heard the telephone ring in the night. When I was younger, at school or church or somewhere, the teacher told us that if the phone rings in the night, it's rarely good news.

Sunday, Monday, Tuesday, Wednesday, Thursday, Friday, Saturday. I was born on a Tuesday. Or a Wednesday.

By all accounts, there was a terrible blizzard. Driving was dangerous. Maybe my mother and I had to spend an extra day in the hospital.

When my sister was born in 1982, I was given a plastic machine gun. The gun was wrapped in Union Jack wrapping paper. In the hospital there was a woman with a yellow cast on her leg. Perhaps that was a different hospital. That night I slept at Andrew Young's house. I woke when it was still dark, built a train track all over the bedroom floor. I think this was the way I dealt with waking for the first time in a room that wasn't mine.

— — —

What is 1982?

A silent movie.

What is silence?

Simultaneously a widow and a bird. Like similar movies, it would have often been accompanied by piano. When Erik Satie claimed to be a phonometrician rather than a musician, he meant that he measured and wrote down sounds. The word 'poet' makes me uncomfortable.

The measurement of sound is contained in migration: the controlled (read: innate) movement of bodies. A collective body. It's an uncommon but good wheeze to stay up all night and rewrite the dictionary. Although I'm familiar with the various parts of speech, I don't consider them close friends. Think about this as an example: it's just as well we stopped at the airport for you to show me the aeroplanes because when we got to the driving range we found it closed for the season.

— — —

I have tried to understand death as related to the idea of waking. I am not certain of the name for this relation. It may be more appropriate to ask somebody better acquainted with mathematics.

We drove to a beach where the rock was said to be rich with fossils. I knew about ammonites and trilobites and harbored dreams of owning a metal detector.

Fossils, like windows, are moments of discourse. Music is distinct from the measurement and transcription of sound. It is a form of recurrence.

I have tried to understand waking as the moment when the world ceases to make sense. Maybe one day everything will be collected in sequence and bound with leather.

— — —

Despite his twentieth century notoriety, Tutankhamen is considered a minor king. I think Frank Sinatra was buried with a tootsie roll, a roll of quarters, other New Jersey artifacts. I keep telling Rohini they should put a change machine in the laundry room. It's 2008 and I'm 29 years old.

According to Sartre the activity of consciousness is a constant reappraisal of the past in the light of a projected future. In this sense, fiction is revealed as the most popular form of immortality. I don't think I'm going to explain this any further.

— — —

I suppose the difference between a house and a burial chamber has to do with windows. Since neither coffins nor sarcophagi have windows, the difference between them is primarily linguistic. I am thinking of this in terms of Saturday and Sunday. Incidentally, it is now Wednesday evening and the pink flowers I bought as buds have bloomed on the kitchen counter.

Tutankhamen's tomb was discovered by Howard Carter on November 4th, 1922. Exactly 73 years later, Gilles Deleuze committed suicide by throwing himself from the window of his Paris apartment. Julio Cortàzar recommends that the reader begin his novel *Hopscotch* at chapter 73. Julio Cortàzar died on February 12th, 1984 exactly 175 years after Charles Darwin and Abraham Lincoln were born.

— — —

I think the Northwest drizzle bothered me less than you because I grew up in a place where the sky was often grey. What I will say is that the West Country clouds and the light pollution from the city of Bristol made the sky look orange at night.

What is night?

It is best understood as rhythm. We gave most of our furniture away.

How we have arrived is as important to me as how we will leave. I realize now that all of our moving expenses were tax deductible but at the time we never thought to save our receipts. In the same way, I am beginning to realize that the biggest question is movement. I mean, the question from which all other questions derive.

Lights' abode, celestial Salem, vision whence true peace doth spring, brighter than the heart can fancy, mansion of the highest king.

It's impossible to tell how long Deleuze waited at his window before deciding to throw himself out. Perhaps the decision had been reached long before he approached the window. In the same dream, I am standing at the side of the road in New Jersey. I have just crashed the car and I'm trying not to lose my balance. There are pink flowers on the median.

— — —

The United States contains at least ten cities of Bristol. Each is in a different state: Connecticut, Pennsylvania, Rhode Island, Tennessee, Virginia, Colorado, Florida, Indiana, Michigan, Maine.

We flew home from Orlando International on July 17th, 1992. I took everything: pamphlets, menus, cups, even a toilet roll wrapped in Mickey Mouse paper. I believed that if I carried these things with me, then they would stay with me, become part of me. I mention this in relation to Frank Sinatra, Howard Carter and the realization that in these rooms inside apartments we are collecting the items that will grant us passage.

This is how Bristol, Indiana exists as the dream of Bristol, England. And America, as it is known, as the waking dream of all who have arrived. What is known as the American Dream is a reduction. The common and singular dream of these dreams simplified into linear narrative. I am trying to write the perfect American story: the book whose name is God.

—   —   —

I tried to tack the cups to my bedroom wall but they wouldn't stick. I tried to find space for these fetishes but could not build a shrine. Instead they were packed inside a cardboard box that my father carried to the attic. Beside the box was a brown suitcase. Inside were the various gifts I received upon baptism, presumably the items I would need for my passage into life. A miniature pewter tankard, a porcelain thimble, a signet ring sized to fit a child, an actual silver spoon.

— — —

Following the Great Fire of London, St. Paul's Cathedral was rebuilt with Portland stone. The Republic Plaza in Denver is constructed from reinforced concrete clad in Sardinian granite. It is the city's tallest building. The equivalent structure in Bristol is St. Mary Redcliffe parish church, a gothic edifice next door to which, in a small house in 1752, Thomas Chatterton was born.

St. Mary's Vicarage, Shirehampton is located in a close off the High Street, next door to the church and across the road from the working men's club. I mention this because the attic of this house contains a brown suitcase and a box of pamphlets, menus, cups, a toilet roll wrapped in Mickey Mouse paper.

—   —   —

Once a month for the three or four years that bridged the 1980s and 90s, we would drive for an hour to go to church with my cousins in Tewkesbury. The church was cold and damp. Above the pulpit on the wall of the nave was the inscription 'All Must Die.'

Rohini asked me why I was writing about death. I said I didn't know and that I was also writing about birth. I said that death seems both distant and inevitable.

The nightly news does not erode this distance.
Watching my blood through a needle into color coded vials does not erode this distance.
The impossibility of a perfect circle does not erode this distance.

I am formulating various ways to achieve proximity, designing rituals to perform over and over. Such is the movement achieved by prayer:

— — —

I ask each rose its bidding then bury my appendix on the lawn.

So I might find it again, I map the garden and pace the relevant distance.

I put the map in a tinder box and bury it with Giotto.

The coffin is tiny, the wood thin and knotted. It is less a coffin, more a box.

There is no coffin: the remains are carried in sackcloth and bound with twine.

Any arrangement can be perceived as sequence, the bridge was built this way. Giotto understood the need for a more efficient passage across the estuary so the various _____s were allowed to bloom.

I ask each rose its bidding and bury Giotto on the lawn.

So I might wake him again, I confuse estuary with afterlife.

God is a conversationalist as well as a father. There are seventeen types of rose in this garden and they all belong to you.

I cradle his head on the lawn.

Past, present, inside. Nothing is getting better or worse. It is only changing.

I do not understand the transition. I hold you until you disappear.

— — —

What is transition?

A movement between states. I am trying to remember the various ways I've understood the afterlife. For example, my uncle explains heaven as God without time.

In Sartre's *No Exit*, it takes the form of what the Eagles sing about in Hotel California — a strange boarding house from which departure is deceptively impossible. Here, the deceased are aware of the living world when a member of that world speaks of them.

Similarly, I believed that when I died my mind would freeze. Whatever I was thinking at that moment, I would think forever. At times when I suspected mortal danger (before a rollercoaster, on a plane) I would think only the best thoughts I could. This still seems reasonable. What troubles me is that I can't remember what any of those thoughts were.

    1982:

Atari distribute a game called Pole Position. Success is attributed to the appeal of driving an Indy car around the Fuji speedway, but the game has a built in solipsism. The situation is a dream of sorts, the movement of the car illusory: the vehicle remains stationary as the surroundings move around it. Our point of entry is stillness. By pressing the gas pedal, rather than thrust ourselves forward, we force the world past.

— — —

There are seven counts of suicide in the Bible, never is it condemned.

I've spent the last four years writing and rewriting a story set in a harbor city of seven huge lighthouses. Inside the story is the apparatus of both Noah's Ark and the Wizard of Oz. In 'apparatus,' I am referring to names and their context. Although this is not that story, I am telling you this so that same context might be carried here.

In the same way, although it is generally agreed that Giotto was buried, the location of his remains is open to debate.

— — —

1982:

Dorothy, a precocious, biblical child, spends her first night in the city. Accustomed to black skies, she mistakes the glow of neon lights for a blood moon. Apocalypse. The Book of Revelation. She informs her babysitter of the prophecy. You laugh.

As she lies awake, her mother is killed in a stationary gold sedan when the airbag inflates erroneously and her skull is crushed against the passenger window. The baby sitter waits in the living room.

I have tried to understand death as a form of movement. I came to the United States on August 11th, 2002.

—   —   —

To heal my shoulder they spread paste across my chest and wheel in a machine to converse with bats. To heal my chest they twist me on the gurney and let moths fly around my temples. On the ceiling, the word 'breathe' is reproduced in several languages. I forget, as I sound the words in my head. I forget to breathe.

I keep appointments every Tuesday and Friday.
I am training my breath to accommodate the new syllables of its name.
I have befriended several moths.
They are healing my shoulder with conversation, my chest with proximity.

The moths die as soon as I learn their names. I hear nothing from the bats but what the machine tells me. They are sending their best wishes, reminding me to breathe.

    1982:

Giotto shoots himself in the chest with an air rifle. The pellet misses his heart.

By the time you force the door to his apartment, he has bled to death over a period of several days: propped on the couch, staring into the television where a woman explains how to make a lighthouse from yarn and shampoo bottles.

— — —

City: the specific angle at which the largest buildings sit in contrast to the land. In England, it is difficult to drive out of the city. That is, after an hour or so, the city you are leaving has drifted into a new city into which you are arriving.

Upon completing Super Mario Land, you begin the game again with an alternate arrangement of monsters. Once you complete the game a second time, you are able to choose where to enter the world. Downtown Denver sits at a 45 degree angle to the rest of the city. I think it's something to do with melting snow.

    1982:

Giotto has the gas pedal.
You should take the wheel.

In the mid twentieth century, one man voluntarily exposed his body to hundreds of impact experiments before finally inventing the first crash test dummy.

Dorothy read this in the Bible.

In Pole Position, even the slightest collision causes the car to explode in the same fractal pattern.

In the 5th century, St. Augustine declared suicide a sin so severe it would keep a soul from heaven.

Game Over.

Giotto was a con man from Omaha, Nebraska.

2. CONTEXTURE

. . . is there a pattern; a theme, recurring, like music; half remembered, half foreseen? . . . a gigantic pattern, momentarily perceptible?

– VIRGINIA WOOLF

— — —

Platelets are tiny bodies that circulate in the blood of mammals. They are derived from cells but have no nucleus. They do not carry DNA.

Central to the process of code breaking is redundancy, the extra information contained in language. For example, in a code based directly on American English, the letter 'e' will correspond to the encrypted character that appears most often. As these redundancies are removed during encryption, the code becomes harder to break.

As we pass Minneapolis, the child sitting beside me on the aeroplane tells me they are stars. The lights of the city, from our altitude: they are stars.

A single platelet's average lifespan runs between seven and ten days until it is destroyed by the spleen. As of 2005, the average life expectancy in the United States was 77.8 years. I was born in London in 1979. As of 2007, this figure had risen to 78.06 years. How long is .06 of a year?

—   —   —

I've never been able to recognize constellations. At least, not as the figures they are purported to be. It always seemed like you could pick any group of stars and superimpose the image of a hunter, a crab, a ram upon it. I mention this because the constellation of Minneapolis, as seen from an aeroplane, most closely resembles a man in repose. There is a needle in his forearm.

It is almost impossible to completely remove redundancies from a sequence. They are present even in coded strands of DNA. I misunderstood this in the possibility that an individual human being may be described merely by incidental information. That is, we could exist as noise, as the redundancies contained in the encryption of something else unknown.

— — —

Every six weeks my blood is drawn and examined because I have an abnormally low number of platelets. The specialist said that my body may be destroying them in error. I have understood this in the way newspapers use the term 'friendly fire.' I have understood that as the overwhelming weight of guilt.

It is important here to consider the difference between mass and weight. .06 of a year weighs in at a little over three weeks. In Andorra, those born in 2007 can expect to live more than 83 years. When they finally pass on in the year 2090, how will the constellations of Denver, Minneapolis, Berlin have changed?

— — —

Three weeks corresponds approximately to the length of time we spent in Orlando, 1992. It was on this trip that I first witnessed not only the game of baseball but also the phenomenon of the wave. In 2004, in North Hollywood, I was employed by a man who claimed that at a USC football game in the late 1970s, he had invented the wave. He had the press cuttings to prove it although I wonder even now, how it is possible to invent something that receives meaning only from context. As if the digit '7' could be credited with the invention of Arabic numerals. After all, in isolation, the wave is just a man standing up and sitting down.

— — —

As a relatively young man, Anthony Burgess is given only six months to live. Aware that his work is incomplete, he sets about writing with formidable verve and commitment. His production continues through this first six months and beyond through years until decades later in 1993, Burgess succumbs to lung cancer in a house in Twickenham, the author of more than 60 volumes of fiction, poetry, drama, essay and biography. Whereas mass remains constant, weight is influenced by the variable forces that act upon it.

That is, driving back from the mountains, I composed my father's eulogy in the taillights of passing cars. As it started to rain, the lights ran and doubled and the eulogy grew plural. All I want is for these echoes to find their origin: the particular measured sound that birthed this sequence. This is my affair with language. Three months prior to our departure for Orlando, at Benny Hill's Southampton funeral, the eulogy was delivered by Anthony Burgess.

— — —

In May 2003, I drove into the mountains with a friend, a retired army Colonel, and a minor broadcast personality to discharge firearms in the Roosevelt National Forest. We ate cold grilled chicken from zip loc bags and drank cans of non-alcoholic lager. I carried a .357 Magnum in a holster, the chicken in my hands and a twelve gauge shotgun strapped across my back.

The Colonel provided the weapons, my friend purchased 500 rounds of ammunition, the media personality brought a single handgun (wrapped in a red handkerchief) and drove us in a pale blue SUV.

What did I bring to the occasion?

A willingness to participate. A foil for the Americans. A canvas on which they would illustrate the things they most valued.

— — —

From the drugstore, I take band-aids and a dark t-shirt with Denver written across the chest. The letters are superimposed over a grouping of straight and jagged lines that I presume to represent the city and mountains. The band-aids offer breathable protection and a non stick pad. The swerve and block design of their packaging is a trademark of the manufacturer, a dated conglomerate who decades ago tried to patent the stomach pump. I take these things so that our lives might perfectly and completely reflect this work.

I do not have a song to sing, nor can I remember the words to yours. Instead, I have burned these initials into my arm so we can sleep side by side in the museum. Of course, reflection is improbable but by noting these correlations we intimate entry into a new chamber, one in which the walls are built of curved mirrors. Most important is the warp created by this curvature.

So, it is a work of becoming?

It is a work of straight and jagged lines onto which language is superimposed. The chamber does not exist in the original pattern but in the curvature that language affords. Such was the response of the patent office. Such is the story of the drugstore.

—   —   —

Midway through *A Confederate General from Big Sur*, Richard Brautigan refers to the 'rivets in Ecclesiastes.' Specifically, this is a reference to his lead character Jesse's method of reading by punctuation. When I started writing this I understood its relation to the preceding although now it isn't as clear. I think I am remembering Erik Satie: reading (as well as writing) can exist as a practice of measurement.

In 1984, when Richard Brautigan took a .44 Magnum to his head he did not leave a widow. He was subsequently cremated, his ashes imparted to his daughter.

— — —

The most popular assisted suicide facility among the people of Great Britain is located in Switzerland. It is estimated that as of October 2008, more than one hundred UK citizens have pursued its services. The only US states where such procedures are legal are Oregon and Washington. A patient must be diagnosed with an incurable and irreversible condition with a life expectancy of less than six months. A physician then writes a prescription for a lethal dose of medication, to be taken if and when the patient chooses.

Oregon was the home of Richard Brautigan from 1944 to 1954, a full 43 years before laws were passed to make assisted suicide legal. Brautigan's body was found in his house in Bolinas, California nearly two weeks after he had last been in contact with anyone.

— — —

I would board trains, not to Bolinas but to Pasadena or back home to Hollywood. On the way to Pasadena the train would pass by what was known in the early twentieth century as 'Suicide Bridge.'

Back in North Hollywood, in the studio where I worked, I would think intermittently of the bridge in Pasadena. Not because of any connection to suicide, but because of its arches, how they would rise out of the tallest trees and fall over the Arroyo Seco.

I want to think of this work as contoured. I want it to rise and fall.

— — —

A dream of falling is said to represent insecurity or instability in waking life. When Pan Am flight 103 exploded over Lockerbie in 1988, police concluded that some of the flight crew may have survived the crash, only to die before rescuers arrived.

In January 1972, Vesna Vulović, a flight attendant on Jat Airways flight 367 that exploded over Czechoslovakia, survived a fall of 33,000 feet. She suffered several broken bones and spent 27 days in a coma.

In January 2001, Abdelbasset al-Megrahi was sentenced to 27 years in prison for his part in the Lockerbie bombing. Now, in 2008, he occupies a windowless room in Greenock prison as the cancer that originated in his prostate spreads throughout his body.

— — —

When Ludwig Wittgenstein designed a house for his sister Gretl, he spent a full year perfecting both the radiators and door handles. The commission from his sister owed as much to Wittgenstein's genius as it did to her concern about his state of mind. When completed in 1928, although the house had no carpets, curtains or lightshades, Gretl concluded that it matched her temperament exactly.

Her concern for her brother was prompted by a twelve month period that began with the death of Frege, continued through Wittgenstein's failure as a schoolteacher and ended with the death of his mother.

At nap time in the gymnasium, when we were to imagine God I saw a man, beardless and smiling, wearing a white gown. His face changed color from red to blue to green to yellow. While working on his sister's house, Wittgenstein dedicated much of his spare time to sculpture.

— — —

On a website where users post questions for others to answer, between 'What does your birthday mean?' and 'How do volcanoes work?' I found 'Have you ever seen a dead body?'

– – –

On January 8th, 1989, less than a month after Lockerbie, British Midland flight 92 crashed onto a motorway embankment in Leicestershire killing 47 people. At school, a week or so later, we reenacted the panic in drama class. During the 1970s, the Wittgenstein House was purchased by the Bulgarian government who restored the building for the use of its new tenants, the Bulgarian Cultural Institute. Because of my low platelet count I receive frequent correspondence from St. Joseph's hospital. I also have to watch out for 'excessive bruising or bleeding.'

In Catholic churches the font is traditionally located at the rear with the altar at the front and tabernacle behind. This is based on the Temple of Jerusalem, organized through the architecture of God himself. During the Eucharist, Christ dwells in the tabernacle at the head of the church. It follows then that the congregation, those that share Christ's blood, become the body.

I'm not sure how this is influenced by cardinal direction, that is, whether the tabernacle is on the east or west wall. What I'm trying to say is that either way, from the window of the Bulgarian Cultural Institute, the constellation we call God is only rarely visible.

— — —

Gustav Klimt's portrait of Gretl Stonborough-Wittgenstein (oil on canvas, 1905) hangs in the Neue Pinakothek in Munich. In the painting, Gretl wears something like a bridal gown. She is standing against a backdrop of grey and bottle green, her hands clasped gently at her waist. At the request of the architect, the walls in her house were painted in a uniform shade of ochre.

In many traditions, white is the color of mourning, the color that follows death. Elvis Presley named his private jet *Lisa Marie*. British Midland flight 92 crashed on what would have been Elvis's 54th birthday. I've often thought that Elvis was able to be Elvis because he was carrying the souls of two men. He had a stillborn twin called Jesse. They are buried side by side in the garden at Graceland.

— — —

Have you ever seen a dead body?

Yes. Of course. And she died in my arms.

Yes. Last September a coworker jumped seven floors to the granite atrium below.

Yes. A man covered with newspaper lying in the road. Much like the face of God, a bruise will change color from red to blue to green to yellow.

Yes. I have held people in my arms as they passed from life to death. There is no dignity. The image of Christ has been observed in clouds, tortillas, x-rays, windows and rocks.

Yes. I was an art student. We dissected a dead person and drew the muscles and bones. The *Herald of Free Enterprise* was a passenger ferry that capsized near Zeebrugge in 1987.

Yes. I asked to see my fiancé as soon as they brought him to the funeral home. It was strange to see him lying there like he was sleeping, knowing he was gone. I stood there and cried, stroking his arm while the funeral director held me up.

Yes. Hundreds. Vietnam. In the moments before drowning, it is said that euphoria washes over the body. Inquiries into the Zeebrugge ferry disaster found that the cargo doors had not been closed when the ship left port. As a result, the hold filled with water causing the ship to pitch sharply to its port side.

Yes. When I was 8, my dad took me on his milk round. The last stop was an old people's home and there was a lady sitting in a chair. I sat and chatted to her. She didn't talk back, but what did I care? I used to talk to my sister's slippers.

Yes. Patients who died while I was drawing their blood. I remember the red ship, resting on a sandbank in the television.

Yes. A man who had been pushed down the stairs by his wife. Someone said he had been beating her.

Yes. I held my stillborn son in my arms.

3. THE DASHES

(A SILENT MOVIE, A DREAM)

I had a feeling of euphoria. I was zeroed in on the glove, but I didn't hit the glove too much. I remember hitting a couple of batters and the bases were loaded two or three times. The ball was small sometimes, the ball was large sometimes, sometimes I saw the catcher, sometimes I didn't. Sometimes I tried to stare the hitter down and throw while I was looking at him. I chewed my gum until it turned to powder.

– DOCK ELLIS

— — —

My prayer book is bound in red leather.
All good wishes to Marjorie from E.M., Christmas 1915.
By January the walk is covered with packed snow.

—   —   —

The first eighty pages consist of three short plays. It is my mandate to distinguish between cherubim and seraphim. Unable to furnish you with data pertaining to snowfall in Pasadena between the years of 1913 and 1916, I will instead report the names of three months: February, April and July. July was the month in which Alfred was killed.

— — —

By Christmas 1915, those in the trenches had long abandoned the singing of Silent Night and returned to the less savory business of war. There is nothing of this in my prayer book but there are several illustrations. A cavalier sits atop a white stallion. Enter THE DASHES.

If consciousness is transparent then white is the color of death. Alfred stands on the balcony and spits at passing cars. What's your name, little bird? The cat balled at his feet.

By January the walk is covered with packed snow. It is singing in the garden. My little bird is singing. The ideal illustration acts as a reflection of the reader. This is Marjorie. Marjorie, Alfred. The ideal prayer imbues a direct relation between the speaker and God.

These are images of a different war. This isn't dynamite, it is a needle. Run your dynamite across my skin and my little bird will sing. It is a nostalgic allusion, a paper chase through Pasadena. On every page a prayer. We gathered the leaves and burnt them.

— — —

These prayers are not founded in the death of God or any among the company of heaven. Insistence on a decisive battle will be retained into the twenty first century. I can offer no illustration but this mirror. Am I to play Alfred? I think so, for now.

In place of logic, may I offer you these trinkets?

Here are my medals. Here is my gun. Her silence is white.
Cut with a dash or needle.
Dear Marjorie: These are my wishes of the season.

By the end of the first day, the British alone had lost more than 20,000 men. The identity of E.M. remains unclear. To my knowledge, no séance took place.

— — —

Throughout the war, Alfred dreamt of a bridge in Pasadena. The city of Pasadena was incorporated in March 1886. The bridge was built in 1913. By July 1916 it was covered with packed snow.

My prayer book lists the names of the dead.
My name is Alfred and I carry a gun.

I cannot tell you these things directly. Marjorie waits in an easy chair by the window. She has pondered a walk through the briars and honeysuckle. The cat is sneezing, and besides, it is January outside. She'd rather spit at passing cars.

What have you brought for me?
The book of Leviticus and two slices of unleavened bread.
For pudding?
A smile.

In this instance, speaker becomes reader.
Her name is Marjorie.
God is a little bird.

— — —

The offensive was ordered by Sir Douglas Haig: his bronze, graven image atop the parapet balustrade. We spoke of consciousness? How it dips toward the object. It is charming to die in the summertime. It is meet and right so to do. The distance from January to July becomes a parenthetical statement of loss. This is the song of 1916. Carry me down to the river, my dear. Carry me down to the sea.

The first car passed the balcony at 8:44pm. A bullet grazed the rear fender, at which point the parade was halted and Haig ushered onto a Learjet bound for Pasadena. Nobody suspected Marjorie, the cat balled at her feet.

My dear DASHES, will you melt with the snow? I have been looking at photographs this morning. The headstones were white and spaced at regular intervals across the field. The City of Pasadena has commissioned a new memorial and we are to write the prayers. Though we are many, we are one body, because we all share in one bread.

My dear little bird, I waited for days at the Cenotaph.

My dear Marjorie, it is possible for the end of a story to occur in the midst of the text. Alfred was killed on the first day of July. I mean, it is possible to die and continue breathing.

— — —

In 1961, Khrushchev uses Yuri Gagarin to disprove the existence of God. Alfred notes the importance of vocabulary: words like skirmish and velocipede.

This disrupts the logic of prayer. The text becomes deranged, split into its constituent parts (though these parts are themselves deranged: one molecule strontium, one molecule zinc). These are weak bonds, the likes of:

> DASH #1   Sticks.
> DASH #2   Straw.
> DASH #3   An old brick shithouse.

After he was born it took Yuri Gagarin 34 years to die. It took Alfred only 40.

In the corresponding illustration, a garden. Alfred leads me down a path lined with pink rhododendron. He has led me this way before. Beneath a yew tree we stop at the bust of a gorilla. Its name is Alfred. We stare at it for days.

Such a prayer is conceived without discernible truth value.
I chew these terms until they turn to powder.

— — —

There was a rumor that 'all' meant 'everything.'
There was a rumor that to breathe was forbidden.
Don't you have a machine that puts food in the mouth and pushes it down?

Instead we improvised plays and performed them wherever we could: in the trenches, on the balcony, once (and only once) aboard the Vostok. Gagarin would whistle a tune by Shostakovich. All would respond, 'Amen. Lord have mercy.'

Such was our habit: to chant the name of God.
Little bird, little bird. Let me in.

A rejected illustration: stallion becomes velocipede becomes bull. The bull seduces a Phoenician princess who flees to Crete and has four sons: Minos, Rhadamanthus, Sarpedon and Yuri. Upon their deaths, the three former will become judges of the Underworld. The latter will become the judge of God.

–   –   –

How are these prayers composed?

It is generally assumed that the process is deciduous. That is, it entertains both recession and succession. We are held in place by momentum, in check by a leash.

What determines division?
As perforation, enter THE DASHES.

> DASH #1   Who is Marjorie?
> DASH #2   Who are you?

On the level of proposition, truth is discarded. Exeunt.

Who are THE DASHES?
As if there could be no alternative reading.

Who are THE DASHES?
They are names. And names are numbers.

Who are numbers?
Alfred's was seven.

Some of the boys pronounced it 'sevarn.' Fourteen had such trouble, he pronounced it 'twelve.' In this way, at age eleven, Alfred was seven but referred to as twelve. The sum of these numbers is thirty. The war was to be over in thirty days.

Is this the argument?

    DASH #3 *(offstage)* Marjorie is the argument.

Marjorie is a screen of transparent whiteness.
A logical impossibility?
A little bird. A prayer.

— — —

On my way to the Cenotaph I saw a woman stooped at prayer in the corridor. Marjorie's hands were filthy. She rolled her shawl for the journey. The rest of the school had been sequestered in the pavilion as the chapel and dining halls burned.

This was recorded as illustration. Acrylic on canvas, September 1986.

What did we lose in the fire? Trinkets, old prayer books. For a while I thought I understood the logic of attrition: aged 40, Alfred fought and died in a war of boys. Yesterday, aged 29, I bought a dustbuster.

Consider this apocrypha: the tallest trees in Pasadena are poplars. All the headstones in Belgian war cemeteries have the same dimensions. The fire began in a waste basket and melted the snow around her window. Of course, the official figure is much lower but that figure is a lie.

A prayer book is a mingling of voices, balled together and thrown at the chapel clock.
My feathers are my body: such will be your Eucharist.
By January the walk is covered with packed snow.

4. OCEANOGRAPHY

(ANTI-TYPE)

What, in fact, haunts me, is the last book: the one we will never write and which all our books try to look like, just as the universe in its becoming each day resembles a little more the pre-existing universe.

– EDMOND JABÈS

Sway is built into skyscrapers, since it is natural to trees.

– LYN HEJINIAN

1

— — —

We assemble at the crematorium on Tuesday morning. As the oldest of the children, it is decided I will ride with my father in the funeral car. When we arrive, the wind is so strong it pops several umbrellas inside out. Until now, this has only happened in picture books.

This is what I think 'submersion' means: one field's absolute disappearance within another.

This is what I think 'field' means: the elemental, whether base or divine. Every civilization has a flood myth. I will tell you ours: May 30th, 1948, the city of Vanport, then Oregon's second largest, is destroyed when the Columbia River bursts its banks. Such are the premises from which we'll begin:

At a yard sale in Tacoma, I find Jackie Robinson's rookie card inside a cigar box. Mint, except the card has been drawn by a child and the numbers replaced by crude hieroglyphs. I buy the card for 12 cents and keep it under my pillow for the next seven years. The first night we sleep together, you find it and ask me what it is. I tell you I stole it from a museum. You say you used to dream about a thief. How he would leave you in the night, only to return days later with scars on his forearms and diamonds in his shoes.

— — —

The original idea was that with every step we would loosen our anchor with the real. The problem was that I never understood what that meant. In any case, the story would have run along these lines:

Amid rumors of a muscular condition that will paralyze her lower body, she is baptized as Dorothy Gale. Initially, it is just a precaution. The next morning we leave Oregon for Kansas.

The journey prompts a correspondence with the Pacific. Although the Ocean is at first slow to respond, our exchange continues for several years. The letters are eventually collected and published under the title *Oceanography*. The volume is available for only a few days before it's withdrawn on charges of oversight and blasphemy. All known copies including the original typescript are gathered and retired to the real hollowed out mountain, served by a secret railroad, somewhere in the Adirondacks.

— — —

I am 13 when Marjorie agrees to tell me the truth. Jackie says 'truth' is the name people give to lies they can't live without. I tell him to go fuck himself and walk four paces back for the next hour.

While the pews empty, I stand with my father as men in long coats line up to shake his hand and nod. I'm wearing my school uniform because it is the smartest suit of clothes I own. It is generally agreed that the service was lovely. At the pub, the egg sandwiches smell rotten. I sneak out to the beer garden and smoke a cigarette in the rain. Taken from Marjorie's purse a week ago in the hospital. I use a whole book of matches to keep it lit.

Prior to 1949, vehicle safety tests were performed almost exclusively with the dead. Aside from more familiar automobile based tests, these early experiments involved pitching corpses down an elevator shaft, dropping steel weights onto their skulls.

In Tamil mystic literature, Lemuria is the sunken continent that connects Madagascar, Australia and the southern tip of India. Throughout the 20th century, several cultists have claimed that Lemurian survivors persist in a network of tunnels beneath Mount Shasta. In every letter, I address the Pacific as Gretl.

— — —

We sit at a stone table and tie bracelets round each other's wrists. When the bracelets snap we pass a teacup and spit in it. When I spit, I see blood in the cup. When the cup cracks, we agree these are good omens.

It looks as if everyone has survived until I notice the dentist. A small crowd gathers round him but nobody can say anything. Jackie is the first to turn away. I want to follow him but it had been my watch. I feel like I should stay and do something. Or at least be present when somebody else does something. But nobody does anything. We just stand there, looking at the dentist and the blood on his right temple. A superpower is a center of gravity. Every book is an account of its own failure.

—   —   —

Inside, I am given a half pint of bitter and a seat with the adults. Across the table is a woman I know from the television, a panelist on a game show in which contestants have to determine the correct definition of a word from an array of false suggestions. I take an egg sandwich and stare at her.

A month later she dies suddenly. The game show leaves her seat vacant for a week before recruiting a new panelist. My father says she'd had a heart condition but I know it was the eggs. Throughout the week, I wait for the tearing pains in my stomach. I speculate on medical procedures that could extract the venom of the egg sandwiches, now for certain in my bloodstream. Perhaps a transfusion will save me. It is unlikely. I make a list of people to carry my coffin from the hearse to the chapel. I make notes to ensure I will be buried not burnt.

It makes the most sense to relate death to submersion. Marjorie says that when you are born you are washed up on the shore and when you die the waves wash over you again, pulling you back to the ocean. I want to be buried at sea but I know this is only for sailors. I think that perhaps I came from the earth, and the earth could wash over me again. The doctor comes to my bedroom and presses my stomach. This is what the sky knows: ash, metal, water, wood and fire.

— — —

As the words come into focus, I realize it isn't a mural but an exhaustive catalogue of the missing. Someone has scrawled over the photographs 'Your silence slit their throats' but the red is too bright to be blood. Jackie says that's what they want us to think.

On an early evening talk show in 1991, former Hereford United goalkeeper and BBC pundit David Icke claims that he is the Son of God. The Korean War memorial in Washington, D.C. is designed so that names of the dead appear as light against dark marble. Which names appear depend on your angle of approach. There is not a possible angle from which all are visible. If there was, the name of this angle would be God.

We sit down in the ruins and Jackie takes a music box from the burlap sack he's been carrying since we left Vanport. He says this is how THE DASHES will reassure us but I don't understand.

Adjacent to the marble wall is a cordoned field of metallic statues. The figures are larger than living men. The shapes of their bodies are distorted by tunics covering the things they have been given to carry. This would become my first letter: Dear Gretl: I am writing because I am afraid.

Typically, recollections such as these are misconstrued. I first caught sight of her through stained glass windows. Her arms colored orange, her neck a deep blue and the twelve apostles danced sadly upon her saffron forehead. She drew my attention away from the vestry. Led it out onto the lawn. I followed her through dusky streets as the last operational lighthouse, suspected of barbiturate manufacture, quietly roused the trawlers.

On May 5th, 1955 a 29-kiloton nuclear device named 'Apple II' was detonated in the Nevada desert. In preparation for the test, the Federal Civil Defense Administration constructed a typical American community in concentric circles around the point of detonation. The idea was to measure, as accurately as possible, the effect of a nuclear attack on an American town. Mannequins were placed in everyday poses. Fresh food was flown in from Chicago and San Francisco.

Dear Gretl: I wanted to show you a photograph of a house that withstood the blast. I wanted to be one of the men who carried the coffin. I wanted to set it down in the chapel, be the priest whose voice did not crack and the organist who played Ave Maria as the coffin was lowered out of sight, the moment when my sisters wept loudest. For years, I experienced a recurring dream in which I would arrive at my parent's house only to find it inexplicably abandoned and reduced to a pile of rubble.

—   —   —

Hypnophobia is the fear of sleep. A largely ignored theory of Atlantis suggests that the lost city was built in the same concentric circles as the typical American community of Irvine, California. Nostophobia is the fear of returning home.

We were engineered so that thoughts would draw halos that would draw the things we wanted to be. We arrived here with fistfuls of small change from defunct Adriatic nations. Denominations so tiny we teetered between worthless and extinct. I know I should be investigating a means of escape. But, in the mean time, would it be inappropriate to lick your wounds?

Dear Gretl: In America all the coins have names: the nickel, the dime, the peacock and foal. I spent a hundred lamplights to stay here but it's still dark when we wake. I say this to suggest that windows are mirrors. That their reflections can be solid, and intimate perfect circles. We are living on a seagull and a farthing but there is no name for what we are. Where we have retired currency: these absences where the light comes in.

2

— — —

From the road it could be a power station, a postmodern cathedral where they will feed us? But it is neither: the abattoir that serves villages all the way from the river to the edge of the woods. This, because we are so hungry, and as Jackie so likes to point out, is our lady fortune in disguise.

My job is to cart the disembodied heads of lambs from the refuse pile to the incinerator in a metal wheelbarrow. I wear a rubber apron and thick black gloves. Jackie says this proximity to death is just what we need but he doesn't say why we need it. I am more disturbed by our proximity to youth. How close to its birth does a lamb need to be slaughtered to still be considered a lamb?

—   —   —

In the house where we learnt music there was a green staircase where ghosts were. The door to the green staircase had no lock but we had been told by our teachers not to open it. At the top of the staircase was a green room with high set windows and old schooldesks. I didn't see a ghost in the room. I saw an open wardrobe and old clothes spilt out onto the desks. A black top hat, a cloak with red lining, white linens.

The next day a man came. He could recite the Gospel of John from memory so we sat in rows in the assembly hall. Sometimes he wore a shroud about his head and neck. Sometimes he pretended to weep. I don't remember much of the Gospel of John, just the man standing at the front of the stage shouting 'Lazarus! Come forward!' It was 12 years later, in the house where Alfred died that I learned how I could talk to ghosts.

— — —

In Page, Arizona, on a street of eight different churches, a car dealership rises where the town fades back into the desert. With the purchase of a new vehicle comes a free goat. But those aren't goats. They are lambs. They are in a small pen on the highway side of the property. There are balloons that mark them there and a banner. Free lambs. And they are alive. This morning I saw a fox running through traffic on 6th Avenue at Clarkson. Every evening we eat offal except Tuesdays when we walk through the snow to Giotto's house.

He fries whitebait in goose lard on his one-ring stove. Once he served us tiny black shrimp he'd caught at the docks with a syringe, a length of carpenter's twine and a net he claimed to have woven from hair. The next morning Jackie sat doubled in the corner of the slaughterhouse vomiting blood into a general issue blue bucket. Some of the others thought this was funny. The floor that we work on, the main floor, they call it the 'blood flats.'

They are driving to the city tonight. A man has come to talk about God and reptiles. I wonder if this is the city we saw from the road, months ago when we were hungry. Jackie tells me a dream he had as a child: I sell everything I own and walk into the woods. I build a house inside an oak tree. Life becomes acorns and silence.

— — —

Dear Gretl: I know that an American book is a book of movement. I know that movement is only seldom accompanied by silence. On her first night in the hospital, Marjorie heard a heart monitor flatline. It was the heart monitor of a woman two beds down on the opposite side of the ward. This is the ward to which I always return.

Marjorie had thought she was dying. But it was the woman opposite who was dying. What disturbed her most was that she could feel no seams as she passed between worlds. Dying felt exactly the same as being alive.

In the morning a man came to consecrate the space that the woman had left. He wore a black top hat and a cloak. He chanted prayers in a language that neither of us knew. Marjorie said that foreign languages could be our secret lives. The man shook ashes over the bed. When he left, I asked Marjorie if she wanted anything from the canteen. The menu was a blackboard and the prices were written with yellow chalk. I didn't eat anything. I just stared at the blackboard. Dear Gretl: This is the tariff that I know by heart.

— — —

Soon we will leave the slaughterhouse. Giotto told us of poppy fields that surround the city. Near the hospital, closer to the water, is the church of Our Lady Star of the Sea. In the park opposite is a miniature golf course that reproduces the various landmarks of the harbor. Here is the lifeboat. The guildhall. The helter skelter and lighthouse. It costs 25 pence to walk to the end of the pier but the helter skelter is free if you don't mind the queue. Before you climb the stairs a man will give you a mat woven from sackcloth. The causeway to the lighthouse is submerged at high tide. Check the times before you leave. Be careful. Check the tides.

Will we meet ghosts on our journey?

Yes.

Should we call our journey a pilgrimage?

A ghost is an impossible literature.
Contained in each unsatisfactory moment is the promise of the next.
Whenever I try to transcribe this conversation, I end up rewriting our story.
A cloud, small as a man's hand, is rising from the sea.

3

— — —

In our various fictions, memory loss associated with a blow to the head can often be corrected by a similar blow. The effect of the initial trauma can be reversed when the act of that trauma is recreated: what was a chance occurrence must become a performance. As such, it achieves what theory cannot, a metamorphosis. Such is the moment when the word is made flesh.

What must be stressed is this duality, the insistence on two events. There is the blow that opens the field, and the blow that either closes or completes the opening.

There was a 17 minute interval between American Airlines Flight 11 colliding with the north tower, and United Airlines Flight 175 colliding with the south.

The interval is one of fertility, of terror and fertility. This is where the book is written.

— — —

The last book I read with my father was *100 Great Lives*, an attendance award from Sunday School. Most received their own Bible. Otherwise, a prayer book. My Bible was black with a cardboard sleeve to protect the pages and a thin ribbon placeholder. My prayer book was bound in red leather. *100 Great Lives* had a bright blue cover with yellow lettering and came with a placeholder that was laminated and red. We didn't finish it. The last book we finished was *The Pilgrim's Progress*. The last great life we managed was Martin Luther's.

There are commentators of Sartre who refer to the past as a mermaid's tail. Something solid, that we must carry as both completion and constraint. Jackie says that by the time the flood catches us we will all have grown like mermaids. I don't know how this will happen. It will just be a fact of our survival.

Dear Gretl: You are walking to a city that is the city within you. Describe to me the architecture. Describe the fountains. The statues and sun. You wake from a dream of loss. The morning is cool and you know the loss is real. Describe to me this morning, the ways in which the city has changed.

—   —   —

Martin Luther is born in Germany on November 10th, 1483. In May 1521, he is declared an outlaw and his writings banned by a Roman assembly known as the Diet of Worms. The assembly makes it illegal to offer him food or shelter. Killing Martin Luther is no longer considered a crime.

We meet him on the road carrying a shepherd's crook but dressed as a mendicant. Jackie asks him the way to the city. He says he will go with us, that we should not travel as two. We must be three.

Dear Gretl: I am writing you the book of my blood. We are together in a liquid text that has grown into the book of my dead.

In Caravaggio's *Beheading of Saint John the Baptist* various figures of his previous works recur to witness the execution. The body is already pale, hands bound at the small of the back and the wound still fresh. A presumed executioner stands over the body, bent at the waist, hand reaching for a clump of hair: the moment immediately before head is wrenched from neck. A woman clutches her temples. A nobleman points to a dull platter. From a window, two obscured figures strain towards the dead man, towards where Caravaggio's signature appears in the blood of the Baptist.

Historically earlier, although later in the story, Giotto's *Feast of Herod* depicts the presentation of the disembodied head to the King. Here, narrative is a horizontal movement written in gesture and echo, culminating at the far right with Herod's reception of the forerunner's head. A drunken promise to his daughter. A precaution against mounting rebellion. The moment of atrocity when the world overtakes intention, when action exceeds capability.

—   —   —

Luther asks where we have come from. I tell him the story of the museum, about the fire and how flames reflected in the animals' glass eyes. The irony of our departure, how leaving was like making our whole lives underwater then being dragged gasping to the surface. This incredible weight: the only part of the story that is true.

In the mornings we see two species of butterfly: the Red Admiral, the Cabbage White. They swarm around Jackie's face and arms. In the prayer book, this is considered a simple omen. He smiles toward the city. We all know but say nothing.

In that moment, as we walk, it is 1983 and Marjorie is showing me the planet Saturn through a powerful telescope. The rings seem ridiculous. My life is completely real.

— — —

The last book is the unwritable book. The book that by its absence enables aperture, the means by which we touch the world. Jackie says that dying is like waking then realizing the life you thought you'd lived was a dream. And from this, instead of a new day, all that begins is your own absence. I have been calling him Jackie but his name is also Alfred. I can carry him no further.

So runs the story of the children who followed Jackie to a railroad in Georgia. How they walked with him to a gold sedan outside the ballpark, rode on the running boards to the station then chased the train until they could no longer keep pace, listened until its rumble faded into the evening, then pressed their faces to the rails to feel its vibrations, to remain a part of him for every possible moment. Luther shares this weight these last few miles. And I realize it is why he is with us. Because he knew.

I have been calling him Luther but his name is THE DASHES.

After his assassination on Good Friday, 1865, Abraham's Lincoln's body traveled 14 days by train from Washington, D.C. back to Springfield, Illinois. His fellow travelers included various dignitaries, hundreds of mourners and the remains of his 11 year old son, William Wallace.

I have been calling them THE DASHES but their name is God.
We bury Jackie among the poppies, in the fields that surround the city.

— — —

I tried to write a book that was the book of our destination. I tried but could not write the city. I could not write the poppy fields or the woods to the east. And so, when I burnt those prayers and wrote the book of my failure, the city came to haunt it. This is how a book of movement can become a book of ghosts. To know them, I stole photographs from Giotto.

Most are overexposed: children in baseball uniforms at a wall covered with ivy. Aboard an anchored cruise ship, a man jumps fully clothed into a crowded swimming pool. In the river, between bridges, a seaplane has come in to land. It is approached by rowboats and the sky is grey.

The photographs were folded inside a letter written in a language I do not understand. The letter was inside a map of a region now submerged. Many of Sappho's poems were torn into strips and used in mummification rituals. Only when the text was fragmented, was broken, could it contain the trappings of death, could it preserve.

There is one more photograph. A woman lies in an open coffin. The room is poorly lit. I cannot look at her without seeing Marjorie. In the weeks after his first wife died, Ralph Waldo Emerson was a frequent visitor to her grave. On March 29th, 1831, more than six weeks after her death, not only did he visit the tomb, but he opened her coffin.

These will be our secret lives.

I fold them inside the letter, inside the map, and burn them.

5. APOLOGIES FOR THE TIN MAN

(A PREFACE)

In the winter of 1986/87, there was an infestation of mice because the crops had not been harvested. So the population of foxes increased. Most of them had rabies, and hunters were called to come and kill them. The wild pigs came back first. Then the wolves. Because people were evacuated, thinking they would be gone for only a few days, they left their dogs. But the dogs then crossed with the wolves and were not afraid of humans. It was very dangerous.

– KONSTANTIN TATUYAN,
former Chernobyl resident

— — —

The transhuman, a _____: a point on the journey from human to posthuman. Which was where the Tin Man froze, waiting for anyone to oil his joints. As luck would have it, a scarecrow and a girl from Kansas but everyone knows this is bullshit. Luck is for the movies.

The transhuman, the posthuman: the linguistic identification of the species is prefixed intimating modification. In revision, the story of the Tin Man frozen on its journey from text to posttext, a _____, something I wouldn't understand.

— — —

The posttext: the text that survives the death of language, a term received from Barthes. The death of language has a green face and dresses in flowing black. Surviving the death of language may be as simple as throwing water on burning straw. Saving one's species from extinction may be as simple as telling stories. Evolution itself is a narrative process. After all, to a mermaid, drowning is the punch line to a joke nobody remembers.

The _____ can inherit genetic qualities that neither parent expresses in a pure species. See, for example, the liger: size in excess of both lion and tiger; unlike her parents, she enjoys swimming. The posttext, too, is a keen swimmer. As life crawled originally from the oceans, so the posttext returns to water.

—   —   —

The liquid text.

The state between solid and gas.

In chemistry, the state bypassed in sublimation: so, a gap in logical progression.

But a gap in logic allowed for by science.

— — —

In the movie, it was water that froze the Tin Man. That is, it was rain, falling on his tin joints causing them to rust and wait. But tin does not rust. And that was not a Tin Man. That was just a man in a suit with a funnel on his head. A flesh man in costume.

_____ity is not a costume, for the human or the text. The _____ text is a naked text (as the Tin Man is naked, covering his modesty with a well placed axe.)

— — —

I am half English and half Welsh. That means that in England they don't like me because I'm Welsh and in Wales they don't like me because I'm English. In America, the _____ of _____ nations, most of the time they don't know the difference. This is the third time I've written about the Tin Man.

There are two bridges that connect England and Wales. And I used to think of _____ity as a bridge, as the overlap or commonality between discrete bodies, then as the name for this unnamable, presupposing of course that everything I encountered could be named, could be known.

My name is Richard. I was born in London to Welsh parents. Now I live in America but I will follow you anywhere if you promise a heart that really ticks.

— — —

There are several nativities of the Tin Man. In the first he is a cyborg, enhanced by the introduction of artifice. In another he is a hybrot: a harmony of the mechanic and organic. He is constructed as such, unlike the movies in which synthetic additions are necessary repairs. The difference lies is the possibility of evolution. The text, as species, retains this possibility. The text, as product, only rusts.

(Hybrots are routinely constructed using rat neurons. Usually, when separated from the body these neurons expire within minutes. Using a sealed dish culture system, a hybrot may live for as long as two years. Likewise, the flightless text cannot sprout wings.)

The third is a love story set inside a hall of mirrors. The mingling here deliberately confuses identity. Although damaged, the image remains whole, as the Tin Man remains alive without flesh, as the text sheds form, sheds clothing. This is love borrowed from conjugal visit trailers. An affair between a Tin Man and a mermaid. The posttext as the resultant bastard.

— — —

The Tin Man had a name. It was Nick Chopper, and he became Emporer of the Winkies. He had another name. It was Jack Haley, and he had a son who married Liza Minelli. And he had another name. It was Hickory, and he worked on a farm in Kansas. Liza Minelli was Dorothy Gale's daughter. Dorothy Gale, whose name was Judy Garland.

The posttext has divorced naming. The _____ is the offspring that can be known and not named. The _____ inhabits the space between screen and projector, where fiction and the listener overlap. It reproduces there and marries and spits names at burning straw. It makes a whore of narrative, forgets the joke but remembers the punch line.

—   —   —

The posttext is the divine text. The transtext (the _____ text) suggests proximity to God. God is a name for the perfect American book. The book of God is written to adapt, to permeate, to ripple. The text of this book is in constant motion, which is how a text exists in water. A text that claims to, of course, by definition cannot.

The _____ appropriates this motion, assumes the properties of fluid. It creates an illusion of flux through shifting paradigms. It is a magician, a conjurer, and a thief. It hides behind a curtain and offers trinkets to visitors. But these are more than trinkets: the _____ manipulates their context. It will hand you a medal, a pocket watch, a scroll and will unfold from your perception of these objects. It will carry you to the river, and swim with what you know.

— — —

I travel on foot. The Tin Man rides a liger. We are paying Liza Minelli a conjugal visit. The _____ suggests mismatch as the thoroughbred suggests incest. She has rolled her trailer to the water's edge.

This is our journey toward the posthuman. The place where thought is intimate but already forgotten: a place of waking. We descend the trench created where the text folds, where the death of language can be glimpsed. The refuse that collects here. The real muck of becoming. The _____ thrives in this obscenity.

Creating such a _____ can be as simple as telling stories. Extinction is the exponential function of death. There are two bridges that connect the human and God. I used to dream of myself as a bridge, an overlap. Now I dream of myself as water.

— — —

The _____ is the transitory form. That is, it is always traveling and will never arrive. This is congruent with certain depictions of hell, but _____ity is not a punishment. Nor is it a destination or target.

How do I resolve the text that cannot be resolved? This is an exercise in reaching out to something that as reflex moves further away. I mean, touching something (a text) that cannot be touched with language. The dangling carrot. The created rock even God cannot crumble. Not a punishment or destination, but a temptation? A reaction to temptation.

How did he resist this seduction? He severed his limbs and replaced them with tin: in chemistry, a poor metal, or post-transition metal. And this is resistance? No. It is surrender. An attempt at survival, resigned to mutation.

— — —

The transhuman, a _____: a point on the journey from human to posthuman. The liquid text made flesh. How can I provide answers when the nature of this text is to question?

I have a destination in mind: fathering the _____ children of Liza Minelli. We will live in her trailer, build bridges to connect Kansas and London, befriend mermaids and ligers and replace our bodies with water. This will be my evolution, with no place for you, Tin Man. My seduction, as absurd as it is strangely comforting.

There is no specific point at which the form mutates, as you are a specific point and your text marks you here. To know you I must leave you behind: to be found by a scarecrow and a girl from Kansas, to stand in the forest and rust.

This evolution, comforting in that it will never arrive.
The posttext, like God, is by definition unattainable.
A gap in logic allowed for by science.
As liquid, we survive by freezing and waiting.

RICHARD FROUDE was born in London in 1979. He grew up in the West Country and moved to the US in 2002. He lives in Denver, Colorado with his wife, Rohini.

www.ingramcontent.com/pod-product-compliance
Lightning Source LLC
Chambersburg PA
CBHW020915090426
42736CB00008B/649